Also by Nicholas A. Price

Poetry Books

AN ELEPHANT IN MY FRONT YARD: *AND OTHER OBSERVATIONS*

THOUGHTS OF YOU: *AND OTHER LOVE POEMS*

FORGOTTEN HOLIDAY: *AND OTHER POEMS*

Fine Art Photography Books

CLEARED HOT!

PLAYGROUND OF THE GODS

HISTORIC ICONS

BRIDGES TO MANHATTAN
and other poetic journeys

by

Nicholas A. Price

A Tough Tribe Book

BRIDGES TO MANHATTAN: *AND OTHER POETIC JOURNEYS*
A Tough Tribe Book
Copyright © 2011 Nicholas A. Price

Cover design by S. J. Harris

Cover images and internal illustrations courtesy of
Nicholas A. Price © 2005-2010. All rights reserved

Library of Congress Catalogue in Publication Data on file with the
publisher

First Edition
ISBN 978-0-9798390-7-8
Produced in NEW YORK
Printed and published in the USA
www.ToughTribe.com

OPM 10 9 8 7 6 5 4 3 2 1

THE JOURNEY	PAGE

Bridges to Manhattan

I want to touch the Empire and Chrysler spears,
Pointing from the earth lined land,
Performances in the clouds, an island dream,
Bulging bends, watered in, underground,
Shadowed sky corridors, confusing corners,
Escaping tubes and delivering spans,
Linking Manhattan wishes,
Hearty goals in yellow speckled crowds,
Linear strokes, shunting my favorite sugar,
Grand Central journeys and platform boarders,
Suburban tentacles, reaching forty-eight,
Alloy birds sunset bound,
Grasping the ground, scraping the blue,
Iced boxes and elevated hopes,
Two way mirrors, reflected pride,
Cycle parks and limousine causeways,
Majestic openings, pencil thin,
Wedges of grandfather brick,
Eyes in the air, towering sun searchers,
Walking and watching,
For some grounded space to call my own.

Under Broadway

Leaving the swarming, five o'clock streets,
I found some space, beneath those boulevard ranks,
Subterranean studies, maps not to scale,
Anatomical destinations, under my skin,
Blood and nerves, water and grass,
Subducted life, weary bones,
Searching for yellow, red and blue,
Manhattan, Brooklyn and Queens,
Traveling on every color, somewhere,
Skipping further, watching the world,
Apple tree roots, reaching for water,
Red lamps on Broad Street, not stopping,
Moving melodies to the Bronx,
Under and over, the melting metropolis,
Dancing in the cars, forbidden,
One-way out, a new adventure,
Checking the alphabet, another letter,
Over the water, under Broadway.

Gardens in the Jungle

I drifted through the gardens, one after another,
Set amongst the jungle, of concrete and glass,
Green acres and breathing space,
Sheltered from radiating rays,
Storage stones, endless motors,
Underground parkers and cold rooms,
Penthouse views, closer to the sun,
Away from the shading trees,
Table tennis and drinking,
Time Square horses, Bryant Park,
A carousel of iconic views,
Sitting, you can only see the tops and clouds,
There is something about the library,
Overshadowed by everything taller,
Without it nothing tall would exist,
Splendid lions and learning,
Back to the Central Park riders,
The thought of water, cooling everything,
Tree walks, grassy flowers,
In the winter I long for summer,
I love watching people exercise,
And never feel guilty,
As they seem to enjoy watching me.

Midway

Wooden limbs and warped wheels
muddled the balmy midway air,
Rollers coasted close to heavy heads,
Searing walls of death,
Deafening the constant banter,
Telling talkers and gabbling gleemen,
Juggled crystal spheres and soaring clubs,
Thrown on a winded whim,
A perilous bill of fare, prepared for cautious diners,
Swallowing blades and flaming pudding platters,
Suspiciously watched
by firmly fixed gyrating girlfriends,
In the custody of skewering daggers
launched by jealous lovers,
Bare bone sprinters chasing,
Gruesome unicycling fools,
Shrieking siblings scamper
into the cover of puzzled parents,
A mass of severed heads, the staple diet of fear,
Pink sugar floss foams at the mouth
of the vanishing lady,
Two-headed marvels and eight-legged fears,
Shocking talent,
Appealing assistants are sawn,
In a sweating magicians repetitive act,
With simply slighted hands and midway marvels.

Strolling Across Atlantic Water

Leaving Mount Mansfield, searching for the sea,
Finding those early birds crying into the snappish air,
Slick ropes slipping, my Portsmouth mooring,
The daybreak zephyr, crowding her willing lungs,
Exhaling, an unsullied first light contribution,
Filling formerly furled sheets,
She was set to wander,
Gently slurping, the salty emerald broth,
Cuffing and drumming enthusiastically,
Pulling the Atlantic swell of Ipswich Bay,
Through the approaching surf,
Pinched persistence, gratifying vigor,
Reaching in the ravenous main,
A relentless course to Pigeon Cove,
No spinning back, dodging Boston ships,
The long way round Cape Cod,
Never snubbing the advance, passing Martha,
Freedom grasped, leaving Elizabeth starboard,
Owned for an instant, as Judith points,
Contradictory forces and focused hearts,
No refined fossils or clumsy clatter,
Resting in New London, miles away,
Strolling back, past the sleeping Jersey shores,
There was the city, across the water.

Broken Bones and Building Cement

Rolling rocks rolled me ragged,
On a cold afternoon of dissent,
Breaking my back of component parts,
Sanding me beached to the floor,
Throwing my limbs, towards Arcadia rocks,
Riding upon the dictatorial breakers,
Gannet gulls gaping,
At my broken bones and building cement,
Lifted and launched,
Jaunting back to shrouded islands,
Foaming with bloodied mouths
Tongued saline sips,
Secretly shelled with stranded scales,
Those broken half houses.

Pelican Pilots

Scraping the snapping Atlantic tops,
Coursing south on custodial tracks,
Storming easterlies, Assateague breakers,
Stoning through crests, a feeding frenzy,
Bumper to bumper, feathered traffic,
Floating fare, prospecting eyes,
Trailing the suspended fathoms,
Sun muddling the silver fans,
Wild horses rising, island currents dwelling,
Swindling shoals and ferocious hunting,
Plotting a long shore parallel,
Pelican pilots, rolling and recurring.

Shells

Day tripping conchologists,
Groomed the sandy belt,
Dreaming of extraordinary finds,
Vibrant optimism, freshly delivered,
Snapping sinking toes,
One hundred and eighty views, a curving globe,
Tackling the hide-tide prizes,
Ahead of the seething treading masses,
Drenched foaming feet, washing weeds,
Saturated tails, missing claws,
Dissected on gale force reefs,
Tipped on the shoreline from murky depths,
Sorted with the shells,
Tumbling stars, urchin spheres,
Stranded with the stinging jelly.

Shells

Across the Potomac

Watching her plunge from a humble birth,
Parting multihued Virginian hills,
Charming autumn leaves and earth water,
Collecting enough color for Atlantic shores,
Journeying past the low white serenity,
Majestic contours and capital decisions,
Governing people, on a peaceful rise,
Emerging from cloudy gray skies,
Remembering those struggling statues,
Organized trees and echoing marble,
Lifting the plying craft, mirroring a queuing sky,
Passed by parallel barriers and buses,
Those late racing commuters,
Bowed heads in newspaper cabs,
Presidential watchers in tranquil spaces,
Tower gazing tourists, broad bridges,
It was nice Harry, but awfully narrow,
Sweeping by, lost forever in the bay.

Galloping Horses

Looming from the languid edge,
Wild mustangs, no riders or reins,
Relentless armies, arriving at lowly sandy toes,
Charging white manes, setting rays,
Breaching and falling,
Calling reinforcements, restoring vigor,
Never waning, always approaching,
Futile evasion, a supreme onslaught,
Knocking the menial strength of human hands,
Crisp autumn leaves upon a chill wind,
No defensive weapon,
To this hypnotic marching mass,
Under the auspices of another world,
Earth burdens upon frothy shoulders,
Advancing creatures, guiding spirits,
Meager grains created, later destroyed,
Effortlessly immersed in the pursuing splendor,
A grain of salt, copious water, lost with eternity.

The Kaleidoscope

Kaleidoscope clams, peppered the Hatteras floor,
Foot written for a moment, rapidly retaken,
Feathered faces fading, ogling the feeding surf,
Cargo stepping, Labrador Currents, trepidation,
The planets emerging, from a clean-brushed edge,
Promised waterfalls and a shrinking world,
Sky needles stabbing, at tall-clouded wisps,
Lighting a path, from the keel cutting diamonds,
Those hardened grounding, merciless shoals,
Crested losses, constant cormorant fisheries,
Resident gulping galleons and pirated mother pearls,
Drawing victims in, over their heads,
For fish fodder and sea lettuce sandwiches.

Rolling Rays

Rolling rays rounded the failing arches,
Rising as the sea met land,
Touched by the passing sun,
Scoffing and stuttering, past the leaning light,
Rallying raiders, a bountiful harvest,
Silver shoals, picking up the powder floor,
Clouding the course, to Cape Romain,
Twisting and turning, almost grounding,
Lifting the scurrying stilts, into the dusky air,
Plucking plovers from plotting paths,
Towards the plentiful plunder,
Into the ingressing bulging breakers,
Over crabby caves, sealed from surging surf,
Pitching promises, towards a hesitant horizon,
An open ocean, boiling with leaping life,
Touring the tributaries, cruising the coast,
Parting circles on the shore,
Swimming for distant seas.

Boggy Peaches

Boggy backwaters stroke the emerald sea meadow,
Savannah slowly studies,
The Southern air slipping, not landing,
Rolling northwards, with the sanded seaboard,
Soft peaches and roadside pecans,
Sweeping bottle green, tobacco miles,
Red cedar reaches and cypress currents,
Sweetgum sticks and knoll builders,
Running into lofty accomplished glass,
Rowed routes, historical pauses, modern plazas,
City chickens, kindling houses on the nettled edge,
Forgotten servants to the rest, mounted mansions,
Tended gardens and nurtured branches,
Succulent streetscapes and vaporous traffic,
Fortress homes and corrugated cabins,
Watched over by Enotah and blue crested peaks.

The Seahorse

Today I held a seahorse in my hand,
It had galloped across the landing sea,
Harnessed by the blustery north easterly,
Searching for a shelled stable on the shore,
Rocky fetlocks and sandy hoofs,
Dune hay and a winded mane,
Trotting with the tyrannical surf,
Shoveling shingle back and forth,
Bridled by the retreating waves,
Beaten back to the rocky reefs,
Sinking into the deep once more,
Saddled by weighty kelp,
Away from the cantering storm.

Battling Beaches

Battling with the beaches, conquistador coasts,
The standing coquina castillo, blunting the blows,
Side sprinters spy every straggler,
Mocking the meniscus, scattering sands,
Fleeing the feasting feathered stilettos,
Darting upon dimly lit dusk,
Dropping deeply, into freshly extracted extrusions,
The inquisitive invaders dispatched,
Sent upon crimped crossings,
Funneled by flickering, soaring sticks,
Pointing patiently, forecasting early earth,
Hiking home, across the warm water web,
Empty handed with the Sargasso swimmers.

Merritt Shores

Tandems rambled, reuniting in storm severed grasses,
Peering from a tangled existence,
Distant compound eyes,
Wide-bodied shadows questioning,
Stranded immortality,
The receding tide tapping the scuttling feet,
Violinists, playing a concerto for a reclusive world,
Taking shelter in perfect parameters,
The fresh golden silk launched, sticky afternoon air,
Snagging a speeding dragon dinner or careless zebra,
Impetuous painted ladies gliding,
Flirting with an earthy spot,
Middle water boiling,
A wild death race of accelerating fins,
Secreted bark bodies, packing cunning hopes,
Skirmishing storks pinching,
Stranded orphans from the silt,
Organized beaked cutlery,
Oblivious marsh cotton and grassy growth,
Moccasin hunters, new territory,
Watched by rolling raptors,
Airborne combat, practicing for a kill.

Into the Deep

Into the deep, through the temperamental surf,
North over gully trenches,
Skirmishing current conflicts,
Some will succumb,
Joining tenants in the basement larder,
Rapacious feeders, eagerly awaiting incoming victims,
Perhaps rescued for a while, netted belatedly,
Hastily returned as spent catch,
The gluttonous fisherman,
Throwing back the small fry, gorging on the big fish,
Distracted delights, sent from the shore,
Skimming sharks content with the spoils of battle,
Dipping back south, the last surviving option,
Resting on dry land for a year,
Surrounded by echo walls,
Then off again for another try,
Eager to make it through this time,
Rising and falling on faraway beaches,
Watching for cutting coral and larcenous shellfish,
Praying for the end of a treacherous journey.

Gibtown

Riverview and optimistic summer gains,
Leafy luxuriant greens, Tamiami trail,
Haunting giants and tattooed ladies,
Octogenarians, six year old tall,
Lobster boy, off the deep end,
Monkey girl, windswept trees,
Roll up to the heaviest man; he has outgrown his lair,
Wearily watching, the vanishing furniture man,
Shifting stamped impassive boxes,
Now you see him, for the last time,
Piped with echoes, flat tones,
Preparing, for time travel,
Fiery-fingered swords and shows,
Dropping memories, larger stories,
The heating and eating season,
Popping corn, fang rotting cotton,
Jetting fighters, chasing lofty air,
Leaving the fogged reaches, across the Alafia,
Discovering a desiccated desert domicile,
Leaving as quickly as culture could,
A moment of magic and marvel.

Swamped in the South

Spinning orbs rolled in endless fair silk,
Cradling my southern jaunt,
Nocturnal acquaintances, never enough,
For all those eager blood seekers,
Cellars surfacing, in misted morning air,
Legless cows and headed cranes,
Black racing indigo friends, stalking,
One hundred mice and walking sticks,
Choral society frogs, flat noted toads,
Pausing for reptilian compositions,
Roaming with armored dinosaurs,
Sharing roadside space,
The carrion sharks waiting,
For liberated turkey and parallel lines,
A tortoise pace, for daybreak tails,
Scrub jays, lost land and endless caves,
Sliding through the swaying lynxes,
Impeded only, by stop light cardinals.

The Short Cut South

The subterranean south travels,
With the departed night,
Darkness cloaking the crossing,
No hat-tipping hopes or parting handshakes,
Sleeping policemen, observing occasionally,
Brightening several spires and humble homes,
Ashen crossed, hillside graves,
Magnolias rain browned, sleeping congregations,
Feather showers, flexible feet,
Missing the drool drizzle gumboots,
Swamp hunters and stationary islands,
Moonless dark eyes and highway grit,
On to the coastal run of sea tears,
Trawled beaches and dead neon,
Shadow creatures and roving cats,
City dogs, small towns,
Famous bridges and notorious rivers,
Diving deep into the diverted depths,
The short cut south.

Drifting with a Lone Star

Exiting the sixty-six at Amarillo,
Cadillac fin ranches and cows,
I am kind to the other drivers today,
Drifting south with the lone star,
Parting those parched corner plots,
Single farmers, solitary trees,
Nodding donkeys and dusted paths,
Towards the lush green, carpet acres,
Longhorn miles and sprouting mills,
Leaning tower homesteads,
Silver spinning sails, hidden water,
Sweaty stacked bales and landed toil,
Stringy vein fences, routes to the heart,
Wood and wire for miles,
Is that a camel in that field?
This is Texas and could be,
To the city lanes and traffic miles,
Towering personalities, in steel and glass,
Slipping to the gulf and Galveston,
Flowing with oil and fenced catfish.

Late on Route Sixty-Six

Overtaken by time,
Languishing in Santa Monica surf,
Gazing at the pride of Pasadena,
Lost time, powdered roadside rests,
Barstow to Kingman, black rock,
The open road climbing,
Everything was mine for an instant,
Capturing rare gas, filling glass and color beckon,
Taking time to talk with wigwams and chiefs,
Out of the darkness, a blue swallow glimmers,
High plains hospitality, respite from winding miles,
Dropping into shamrock, passing the milk,
A broken break, fighting the Arkansas flow,
Eleventh Street Tulsa, a new state and city,
Water for man and fuel for horse,
A field of green for grazing,
Space for my weary carriage,
Gorging miles, Galena boarded,
Following a trail hard won,
Parallels and hesitant bridges,
Skirting mountains, filling valleys,
Eureka, I had reached Meramec,
I could only walk the Chain of Rocks,
And drive on to Chicago,
Crossing the land, taking more to conquer,
Dissected and bypassed, nature and wonder,
Arriving everywhere, behind schedule,
Still in love with route sixty-six.

Stovepipe Heat

Stovepipe heat had me baking with the blondes,
Open-air freedom on a Friday afternoon,
Saguaro spines, cloud searchers, pointing somewhere,
Web curtains and Diamondbacks at my feet,
Trapdoors for strangers in unlocked space,
Continuing to climb unabated,
Tuneless organ pipes, no fanning breeze,
Once beloved cacti, now hunted wet flesh,
Scorching with the earthen ground,
Barefoot rocks and no camel bridges,
Journeying with the constant compass,
Parched prehistoric wells, a puddle would suffice,
No corridor escape, marked exit here,
Fire alarms and scorched walls,
Drifting with winter snow, shelves of water,
Glassy springs, great lakes and river rafting,
Sailing on the fresh sea of an April shower day,
Resting in supple silver tubs,
Bring that winter rainfall,
Pour it over this desiccated dirt,
Let me shiver for a while.

The Iron Backbone

Grand Omaha goals, taking Iowa under a wing,
Sacramento beckons, Minnesota grains,
The work of Wisconsin, Michigan and Ohio,
Hauling the weight of Idaho and Illinois,
Slicing sharpened peak and filling level plain,
Wyoming coal, lighting Saint Louis,
Tripping over rivers, drinking thirsty streams,
Hoarding the elixir for lonely desert tracts,
Focused dreams and distant horizons,
High into Colorado, on to Salt Lake,
Staring toward the forging goal,
Hard won battles and righteous tasks,
Filling Dakota trucks, reaching Montana skies,
Breaking rocks and satisfying valleys,
Spinning daydreams into truth,
Blue grass riders, San Antonio ranchers,
Triumphing with Memphis and Little Rock,
Overlooked by the passing world,
Flying across parallel lines, planetary borders,
Kansas to Tucson, on to Seattle,
Fifty thousand miles of united legacies,
Stone and steel, upon her back.

Foot Printed Sand

I had the only room with a bookshelf,
It had books, weekly pennies saved,
The pacific coast highway scrapes the top,
Foot printed sand, lost party balloons,
I was happy to sit with gulls,
Breaking from desiccated desert days,
The listed people could wait,
They could roll up their red carpets,
Forget the clattering cameras,
Stroll barefoot here instead,
Park those padded cars somewhere,
Probably a beach premium,
Or have the chauffeur drive around,
A city block or two,
Glued to Los Angeles streets,
Send him searching for a bucket and spade,
Sand castle builders in penguin suits,
Fashionable gowns in rolling surf,
We could chat casually, discussing shells,
Hermit crabs and real estate bargains,
Find a home, just the right size,
The sun sets on the Malibu shore,
Encouraging daydreamers like me.

Cascading Dreams

I scrambled down, Columbian steps,
Cascading over, a changing land,
Jumping through, the ring of fire,
Upon the shattered trees, of hotter days,
Reshaping the rise, starting below,
Coastal spines, clouding crater lakes,
Washington, with Oregon rowed,
Mirroring mounts, over Trillium Lake,
Hemlock towers, insatiable thirst,
The Ponderosas brooding, in chaotic crags,
Rain shadowed slopes, with cinder cones,
Coughing, with habitual fumaroles,
Steaming, from earthen voids,
Boiling, in the depths of devils kitchen,
Pots of California, mud pie,
Delivering hot rock, promising cold winters.

The Olympic Winter

It was an Olympian love, for those snowy peaks,
Drizzling jungles and skyscraping cedar,
Spotlighting the musing glacial windows,
Protecting the west from stacked seas,
Sugar powder and snaking wires,
Breathing ice breezes, scraping borders,
Folding to the peninsula of treacherous coasts,
Flattery masking, the austere sea pillars,
Captivating a cuffing swell,
Joining Juan, for sunsets over the strait,
Melting snow tears on pacific air,
Sailing the other way round, this time,
Olympus observing the majestic deep,
Reaching the shore, with snow fed arms,
Wearily rising, waiting for the world.

The Seashore at Badwater

Sundown shadows mask a pulsating palette,
Standing here upon the swept shore,
Tangled mesquite driftwood,
The tide at its lowest ebb,
Tapping the feet of proud capped mountains,
On the other side of this lonely ocean,
Promising an end to my parching thirst,
In this mendacious rock sand sea,
A thimble of tears would suffice,
The only thing floating is my imagination,
A billowing sail, rounding the cape,
The echo of gulls and lapping waves,
A child's playful voice, stamping on sand castles,
Life cries in this untamed wilderness,
The daydream broken, the raven reminder calls,
I would be carrion without water.

Maahunu Behind Me

Maahunu behind me, the Timbisha forever scattered,
Mere dust, on the flanks of the searing breeze,
Stroking the peeling white coat,
Death Valley Junction,
Standing as a memento, heydays and restless rail,
In sight of the ash black range,
The funeral mountains and beyond,
The darkening cloak, disguising a dreadful dagger,
The wanton flats, a proving ground for gravediggers,
Scorching an earth,
Previously toasted by the merciless sun,
Mortals brawling with outrageous power,
Spilling over into a stark wilderness,
Freckled by the frequent trailer dwellers,
Tolerating fiery heat, planting straw roots,
Drawing the simple liquid from below,
Amid the curious creosote, mysterious mesquite,
Quenching an endless desert thirst,
Crimson ochre, Panamint forgotten,
Joining a sapphire sky,
Postcard pictures overflowing,
With the fleecy clouds masking,
The expanding mushrooms of an earlier time.

Fremont Street

Failing neon, crushed rebellious hopes,
Check cashing time, slots filled,
Ten-dollar timepieces, motel backs,
The future starts here with zebra strollers,
Blackjack and financial aid,
Bakery chips and hard rollers,
The past pouring down, Fremont Street,
Everything reasonable under the moon,
For talking pigeons, sidewalk sprinters,
A cornered hacienda and shadow sculpture,
Gap desert teeth, stalled trailers,
Safari promises, ranching a cobalt sky,
Dice throwing dialers, day laborers on hold,
Lucky dealers with roulette promises,
Atomic parties, weekly tariffs,
Cut-rate walkers, society cleaners,
Balcony whistles and heated buses,
Lights never changing fast enough,
For fantasy callers and people watchers,
Broken carts stacked with life possessions,
Overheated radiators and stretched thermostats,
Repainted promises, added benefits,
Barrel bottom scrapers and rewound cars,
Mattress stack stains, pallet dealers,
Ending with a dream, an angel with hourly rates.

The Western Homestead

Scorpions sprinted across my desolate carpet,
Clambering over nomadic furniture,
Shrouded by wall hung oil,
Frozen tarantulas crept in with her Cadillac,
Hiding beneath, my stranded Lincoln, mark five,
Ants ignored every boundary,
Approaching and leaving, with no invitation,
Slipping under widowed fences,
Sidestepping, ravenous reclusive caves,
Claustrophobic lizards, scaling my walls,
Peering in on nocturnal disorder,
Waiting, as Crotalus rattled my threshold,
Refereeing the boxing Kangaroos,
Liberty, for transient coyote cubs,
Watching budding olives in a cacti patch,
Eavesdropping on humming birds,
Searching, high and low for buzzing cicadas,
Cloaked with the mantis,
Continuing to pray with passers by.

Rattling Trains

Bombarded banks and persistent rattling continued,
Not a single sight of steam,
An inch of tarnished track,
A fenced station, a solitary class, no tickets,
The apathetic caboose stranded,
Stolen wheels on gritty earth,
Protracted walks to Tonopah, twice as far to Ludlow,
Bridges down and grade roads intercepted,
The bitter river, lost deep below ground,
Flash flooding offering, the only chance of revival,
Sending torrents tumbling,
From the golden bullfrog hills,
Scramming safes washing down stream,
Pilfering crumpled paper, every yellow coin,
Lifting the lowly wooden cemetery,
Changing the plots,
Leaving the hard moored jail,
Close to the house of ill repute,
Vacations high and dry at the open-air school,
Time to clean the dusty shelves,
The absent backbone of Porters store,
The drunkards' house stands firm,
Taking every drop to build,
The mercantile general, glued in place,
Praying for provisions, a purchasing public,
Winding roads to nowhere,
Flowing from a forceful mass,
Streets of half built horizons and rattling trains.

Shimmering Water

Sugary stretched valley seas,
Reached to the wilderness beyond,
Rolling flat and glistening,
Lake lifting hopes of abating heat,
Cooled drinks and a resting place,
Weary feet at the irrigated edge,
Tidal flotsam under foot,
A basin ocean beckoned,
Two hundred and eighty below,
One hundred and twenty above,
The peering peaks searched for meager tears,
Not another smoldering round of golf,
With the crusted devil,
As white-capped Whitney wept,
Scuffing fresh elevated clouds,
The twenty mule teams rested,
Furnace cooking in the creek,
Racing continued on the playa, thirst unnoticed,
The Armargosa failed again,
Unable to break the surface hexagons,
Taking her bitter offerings,
Bleeding into Grimshaw Lake,
Sustenance for biting bugs,
Overnighting trailed feathers,
Fostering dreams of promising treasure,
Slabs of gold and hot water bathing,
Cutting the soft dry land,
Indulging swelling ranch dates,
Leaving the barren borax,
No hope of shimmering water.

CITY GARAGE

Unnatural Causes

Quarrels crammed a brimming crest,
Seventy-two carcasses high,
Crumbling rocky markers, unnatural causes,
Six thousand feet and a hundred more,
Cut from the hemp,
Planted deep beneath and far behind,
The heaven or hell division,
Never permeating, good judgment ground,
Handed down at the million dollar courthouse,
Rattling raging saloons, troubled red light corners,
Confined cabins and a lengthy stroll to the outhouse,
The final opus voiced, at the humble opera house,
Flickers boxed, at the bleak boarded gem,
Murmuring clouds, clutch silvery hopes,
Stagnated promises and routed riches,
No longer travel,
Drawn from the earthy cliff, across a bottle green sea,
Creaking tinderbox hands and contrived iron,
Floating gantries, empty sheds packed with pests,
Bricked towers pinning, scenery to the earthen skin,
Platted out with nothing but no trespassing,
Overgrown dealers, rejecting new models,
Shadowed by the soaring sentimental slope,
The stalled world of the tamed west.

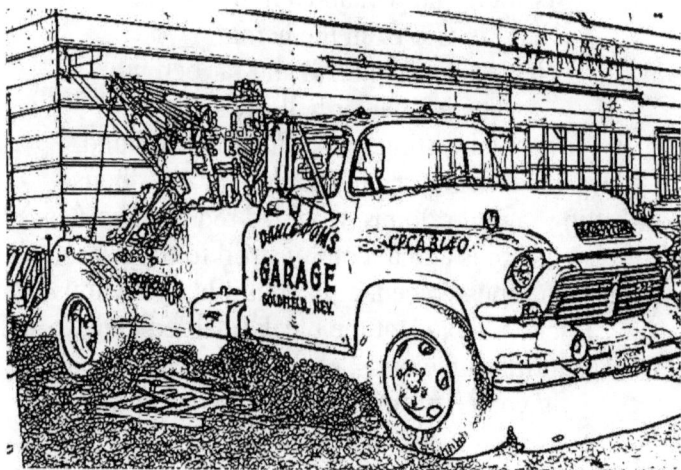

Esmeralda Gold

New gold bakes in Tonopah tankers,
Jetted terrain defended, big horn lairs,
Feuding feudal mountain barons,
Won with an ace, built on bullion buckets,
Forging promoters, shoveling prospective earth,
Lovely ladies two a dozen, expensive options,
Burned in a hat architects afternoon,
Built and razed, driven through, with no fuel for miles,
Leaving hot haunted hotels and a hanging courthouse,
Murder at the Mozart club, a tiffany defense,
Boxers dueling, never returning,
Empty schoolhouses, claiming jumpers hung high,
Buckling playing-card banks, tombstone gunslingers,
Parting with broken down breakdown trucks,
Joshua besieged, garages without cars or pumps,
The oldest saloon, open to mules and fools,
Marking matchstick houses and wooden plaques,
Impoverished signs and improvised spelling,
lead the way,
Soaring blue skies and lowly graves,
Taking simple plain earth,
Searching the high paying dirt,
As march hares fool on a hillside of posted claims,
Dreaming of Esmeralda gold.

Secreted in Eldorado

Secreted from civil conflict,
Pinched toward roasting retreating rock,
Simple mercenaries, fleeing the fray,
Discovering a harsh hideaway,
Nineteenth century hopes, misplaced new aged planes,
Pointless dreams, thirty-cent gas, inoperative pumps,
A littered land, dropped from above without a care,
A coated chaos of seized apparatus, slain sedans,
Filaments of superfluous birds, oxidized pledges,
A solitary school bus idles, no youthful prospects,
Sun-dried tailings butter spread, flooded emulsion,
Scarring the sienna earth,
Sketching a course for convening packs,
Ravenous winders relax, on a drafted breeze,
Rocked edges echo, the continual chewing chant,
Thwarted diggers linger, within the golden earth,
Lost battles with sizzling scorpions,
Coated canvas, a game of chance,
Complimentary admission to an affluent grave,
Delivered deprivation, no return trip,
Deserted by the fatigue, the bloodied frontline militia.

Spanish Travelers

Shadowy pack trains stood stationary,
Larger than life in the noontime sun,
Shading beneath a few cotton wisps,
Close by, the ominous crimson cliffs,
A Western struggle, resting rattle and parched pony,
Conquering a land unprepared for discovery,
Bothersome burros, ambushing sparse supplies,
Lone torch yuccas, flaming floral hopes,
Tumbling weeds slipping past,
A gentle breeze, struggling seeds,
Joshua stands in solitary confinement,
Offering confused directions,
Snaking paths sliding to distant calico hills,
Landscaped views, zooscopic eyes,
Mammoths rambling with extinct promise,
Wallowing in a muddy chasm,
Amid the surfacing cherry cream sediments,
Looming conical skins, spotting the sagebrush basin,
Primitive civilization, sustaining sparkling tears,
The lofty ponderosas stand mocking,
Lapping the final juice of down pouring streams,
Distant matchsticks,
Running with the Spring Mountain range,
Carrying dry pinions high into the plain aired sky,
Distracting minds from creeping barbs,
Gripping in a resting second,
Ready to roam with the Spanish travelers.

The Blunted Colorado

I watched the ashen powder roll,
Sun tripping from Colorado crests,
Cutting down and grinding ancient ground,
Running on sedimentary sands,
Fresh ravines and toppling towers,
Opening an earthen wound,
Slipping on to another land,
Lighting the sky and three deserts thirsty,
Drawing hungry city straws,
Badlands and beaches, washed valleys,
Overton echoes, misplaced towns,
Muddy mountains and virgin rivers,
Burning my hands, on blackened flows,
Slipping with gypsum ledges,
Exposed with quail in eagle sight,
Scurrying antelopes in big horn space,
Dawdling for deliberate walls,
Forced to the corners of human concrete,
Borrowed and taken,
Sprouting those California fields,
Hot springs and basin buckets,
Leaving nothing to fill the ocean.

Wigwams and Rusty Dreams

Wigwams and rusty dreams,
Routed on sixty-six,
Stopping for a minute, never leaving,
Paralleled union rail and discount batteries,
Conical concrete, Chevy and Ford,
Sleeping in the past, fin and contour,
The last bastion, amongst the ancient paint,
Drifting with Fairlane and Bel Air thoughts,
As the future drifts on by, somewhere,
Far from the freeway of big boxes,
Ten lanes, twenty-four hour gas, faster food,
On the move and eyes advancing,
Interspaced by intersection,
Sleeping lodges, chained,
Themed parks and no trees,
New state welcomes, weighted trucks,
Limited speed, no overtaking,
Enticing diversions on every board,
Rushing ahead, they missed this one.

Six Miles by The Lake

Six miles by the lake, shadows over ripple water,
Metropolis and steel, rising from sanded dunes,
Dinosaur scrapers, repossessing the crusted ore,
Through the folds and banks, Monday baking,
The molten cloth of giants,
Thrown from the loom on Tuesday,
Pounded into the shape of humankind,
Nuts and bolts for a hungry earth,
Finished by Wednesday, sweating brows,
Rusting by the damp air shore, every Thursday,
Creased and rolled, out to Friday pasture,
Awaiting news from Pittsburgh towers,
Rinsing blackened hands,
For weekend rest on Beverley Shores.

Windy Lakes

Three hundred miles of Michigan,
Drifting over a landed sea,
Millions more on this old DC,
She looked like the first off the line,
We had got to know each another,
After only a few thousand,
Sweeping down, to a candlestick metropolis,
Searing towers, smaller sisters,
Pushing forward on the hawk wind,
Scraping clouds, with city brothers,
Paddling for a moment, on inland shores,
Feeding the Mississippi, lifeblood rivers,
Thinking of her next call, abandoned in the desert,
Away from winter winds, traveling blues,
An everlasting vacation, dry leased,
Remembering ocean sunsets and Chicago skies.

Clouded vision

Steam thrown billows, scented fiery ash,
Doubtful day tripping dreamers,
Soaking in secondary sweat,
Fireboxes and childhood dreams,

Hardened footplate forgings,
Toiling servants, tough tyrants,
Rations for a winning ensemble,
Stokers without a conductor,

Setting out, rambunctious and assertive,
Gathering speed, approaching,
An infant of discovery, testing constitution,
Vocal chords extended,

Climbing, loud and obnoxious,
Shovel pace, wheel speed,
Onwards and forwards, ahead and beyond,
Human racing, esteemed creations,

Downhill yielding, a slowing conclusion,
Leaving in darkness and on to the next,
Weeping over lost adventures,
Fifty states and clouded vision.

ABOUT THE AUTHOR

Nicholas Price is a poet whose work has been published through a series of bespoke and mainstream publications and books.

With a legacy of work now collated and published in several new titles, bringing a unique poetic style and perspective to a wide range of subjects enjoyed by all readers and ages.

His poetry, writings and photographic work have been exhibited at key events and institutions. The acclaimed collection titled *Cleared Hot!* – a photographic story and essay - was acquired by one of the world's most prestigious institutions, the United States Library of Congress.

OTHER AVAILABLE TITLES

America is a way of life and a state of mind, to be savored and discovered.
Nicholas Price celebrates this beauty and diversity through his poetic artistry. His journeys take us from the Bridges to Manhattan to the pioneer trails of the West Coast and beyond.

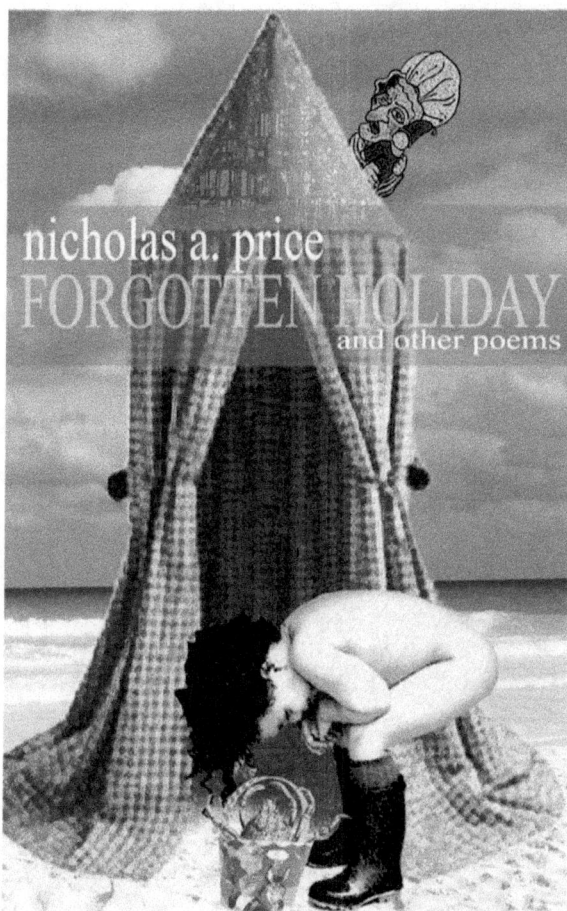

nicholas a. price

FORGOTTEN HOLIDAY

and other poems

Nicholas Price takes us on a poetic journey through childhood and life experience.

Nostalgic, amusing and a must read for those who sometimes question; "whatever happened to the world we grew up in?"

Forgotten Holiday is one book to keep amongst your own treasure trove of memories.

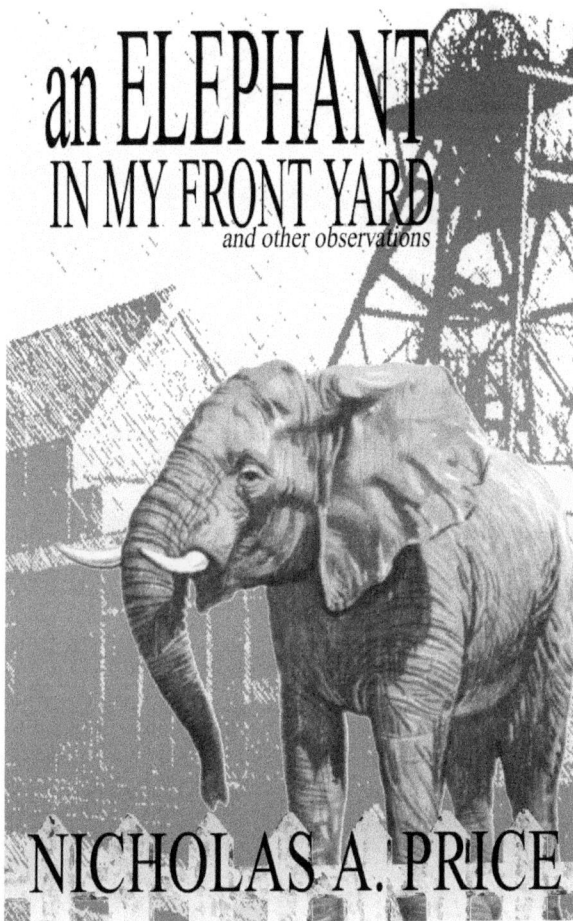

an ELEPHANT
IN MY FRONT YARD
and other observations

NICHOLAS A. PRICE

Nicholas Price presents his frank and sometimes humorous poetic
thoughts and observations on life.
From social and political change to the hopes of us all.

Described as "a refreshing new voice in poetry", these works are
timeless and reflective of the world we once knew and the one we
have become.

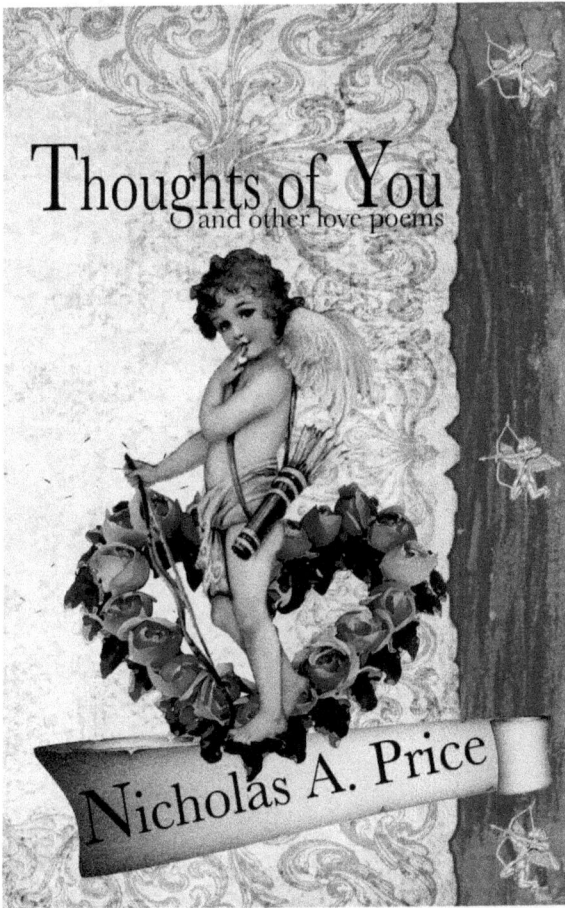

Thoughts of You
and other love poems

Nicholas A. Price

How would you describe being in love to someone who has never experienced it?
Poet Nicholas Price pens the human storms of desire, heartbreak and devotion.
The distant yearning to unyielding passion, absence and infidelity, grief and solitude, those erratic and chaotic emotions we call love.